Testimonials

I speak both as a teacher and a parent who personally experienced Dr Mankes's expertise. Dr. Mankes has the patience and the talent to work with children. She helps children who need extra practice developing their fine- and gross-motor skills. This also aids in enhancing their self-esteem. Not only did my son succeed in increasing his fine-motor skills with her, but many of my students did as well. She is the best occupational therapist in town!

PK, Teacher and Parent

As a teacher who works with students with special needs, I highly recommend Dr. Mankes. Her patience, knowledge, and expertise give students results and confidence!

2nd-Grade Teacher

Carol is amazing! As an educator with over 15 yrs. experience and a Doctorate Degree in Educational Leadership, I have been thoroughly impressed with her ability to relate to each individual child, meet him/her at his/her educational level, and provide the necessary help for improvement. She is not a labeler, but rather a fixer. She has the educational expertise to make a difference in children's lives, and she is also somebody whom children love! I highly recommend her.

School Director of Education

Doctor Carol Mankes has been a wonderful gift and blessing! My 7-year-old daughter really struggled with writing, so we hired Dr. Mankes for private in-home OT classes to improve her handwriting, grip, and strengthen her hand/arm muscles. We got so much more than that! Not only did Dr. Mankes help improve my daughter's grip and handwriting in record time, but she also helped improve her confidence and self-esteem. She also helped her gain independence while also strengthening her fine-motor skills. My daughter looked forward to the twice-weekly classes with Doctor Mankes, she became proud of her accomplishments, and has improved tremendously. I highly recommend Dr. Mankes; she is exceptional in her work; and she truly cares about the kids she works with. She takes pride in their improvements and enthusiasm! I felt a genuine affection for the kids she works with, like my child.

Parent to a 7-Year-Old Daughter

We started our journey together 3 months ago when my 3.5-year-old son's teachers expressed their concern about his fine-motor skills and his language development. Since our son stayed home with us for almost a year during the pandemic, and since at home we speak only Hebrew, we wanted an Occupational Therapist who speaks Hebrew as well and understands the complexity of the situation. Carol assessed our son, provided a comprehensive report, and explained her insights and plan for treatment in a clear way. Our son loved Carol from the beginning and connected to her very quickly. This is a very important quality you wish to get from an OT. Carol works not only on the specific challenge the child encounters, but also on various emotional aspects like self-esteem, self-confidence, etc. Carol also sends an informal report after every session, which helps us getting involved in the process as well. Within a few weeks, our son improved his fine-motor skills, his English language skills, his social behavior, and his self-confidence. And all with a lot of smiles and laughs. Our son looks forward to every session with Carol. The teachers are amazed by the progress he has made.

Parent to a 3-Year-Old Son

Dr. Mankes has been a great resource for my practice! Carol and I met at the Jewish Day schools over 10 years ago when we were both servicing the children on site. Sometimes, the children needed both Psychotherapy and Occupational Therapy, and we had a chance to work as a team. This teamwork brought so much growth to the students and to us that we still connect to work through challenging cases. Carol is a very knowledgeable and sensitive professional that is passionate about her work and the individuals she wholeheartedly wishes to help.

Mental Health Counselor

I have two boys, ages 7 and 11, who've had trouble with their fine-motor skills and was referred to Dr. Mankes by both of their teachers. In the last year I have seen a huge improvement in both, especially with their handwriting. Not only is she incredibly knowledgeable in what she does, but she also quickly made both my boys feel comfortable and happy when working with her. Thank you, Dr Mankes, for all you have done! We are lucky to have found you!!!

Parent to 7- and 10-Year-Old

Carol is a skilled therapist, as well as a lovely person. I worked with Carol in a school setting and was able to see her gift with children, as well as the results she achieved.

Speech Therapist

On the Road to *Handwriting Success*

A Resource Guide for Therapists, Teachers, and Parents

Dr. Carol Leibovich-Mankes

Copyright © 2021 Dr. Carol Leibovich-Mankes
All rights reserved.

No part of this book may be reproduced in any manner whatsoever without the prior written permission of the publisher, except in the case of brief quotations embodied in reviews.

The views and opinions expressed in this book are those of the author and do not necessarily reflect the official policy or position of Halo Publishing International. Any content provided by our authors are of their opinion and are not intended to malign any religion, ethnic group, club, organization, company, individual or anyone or anything.

ISBN: 978-1-63765-124-7
LCCN: 2021919704

Halo Publishing International, LLC
www.halopublishing.com

Printed and bound in the United States of America

I dedicate this book to all the family and friends who have supported me throughout my career, loved ones I have lost who will always be remembered, and my daughter, Arielle, who has been my teacher and rock on our life journey. She is also my inspiration for the strong desire to provide other parents with the tools to advocate for their children who are struggling with handwriting and/or learning-related issues.

Contents

Who Can Benefit From On the Road to Handwriting Success	11
Foreword	13
Introduction: Handwriting Basics	15
Section I The Road—Foundational Components	17
Chapter 1 The Nervous System	19
Chapter 2 The Sensory System	22
Chapter 3 The Musculoskeletal System	36
Chapter 4 Cognitive & Perceptual System	38
Section II The Vehicle—Performance Skills	41
Chapter 1 Gross-Motor Skills	43
Chapter 2 Good Posture	51
Chapter 3 Fine-Motor Skills	54
Chapter 4 Visual-Motor Skills	62
Chapter 5 Visual-Perceptual Skills	65
Chapter 6 Visual-Acuity & Oculomotor Function	69
Chapter 7 Executive Functions	72

Section III The Driver—Task Performance   74

    Chapter 1 Pencil Grasp   76

    Chapter 2 Writing Posture   78

    Chapter 3 Handwriting Rules   80

Section IV Mechanics—When to Seek Further Assistance & From Whom?   85

Appendix A: Examples of Inefficient Grasps   89

Appendix B: Examples of Handwriting Improvement   95

References   99

About the Author   103

Who Can Benefit From
On the Road to Handwriting Success
A Resource Guide for Therapists, Teachers, and Parents

Parents

Parents can use the information in this guide to assist in the development of their child's handwriting and determine when it may be beneficial to obtain further professional assistance.

Teachers

Teachers can use the information to further develop their students' handwriting within a classroom setting and feel more at ease referring a student for additional outside assistance.

Occupational Therapists

Occupational Therapists will find this an excellent resource. This guide can be used for therapy sessions, home programs, parent education, and/or self-enrichment.

A Powerful Learning Tool for Others

Parents and professionals alike will find the guide an excellent learning tool to address a variety of handwriting difficulties and navigate the world of handwriting development and overall learning.

**SKILLS AND STRATEGIES
FOR HANDWRITING &
OVERALL LEARNING
SUCCESS MADE SIMPLE!!!**

***DISCLAIMER: Please note that information and activities provided in this guide are designed to promote your child's typical development and are not a substitute for therapy. If you are concerned about your child's skill development and/or overall learning, please contact an Occupational Therapist or other professionals as deemed necessary!

Foreword

Imagine yourself driving down a newly paved street, in a sturdy car, and being familiar with the driving rules. Most likely, you would feel confident that you could successfully reach your destination, right?

Now, imagine the opposite is true. You are still aware of all the driving rules; however, the roads are bumpy and cracked, and your vehicle has a few mechanical problems. Would you still feel as confident and relaxed about reaching your destination?

Most likely, the average person would be less optimistic in the second scenario since the road and the car are in less-than-optimal condition. This situation could possibly compromise the driver's ability to follow the rules and reach his/her destination successfully.

Although it may sound strange, completing a handwriting assignment would present itself quite similarly. Imagine a child named Tommy having to write an entry in his class journal. He is sitting in his chair comfortably, holding his pencil, able to concentrate, able to transfer his thoughts to paper, and aware of the handwriting rules. Tommy can complete the assignment easily. The road to completing his assignment does not present any obstacles.

Now, imagine a child, Jessica, who needs to complete the same assignment and is familiar with the writing rules. However, unlike Tommy, she has a hard time keeping herself seated upright, holding the pencil hurts her hand, and she is feeling fidgety. Jessica sets herself to complete the task, but her handwriting is illegible. The assignment is not completed successfully.

Why the difference in results when they both knew the rules? The difference is that Jessica did not have the stability that Tommy had. Jessica can be compared to the driver who did not have confidence in the road and his vehicle. Her lack of stability ultimately distracted her from achieving her goal in the most efficient way possible. Jessica's deficient skills did not allow her to navigate the road easily, and therefore her ability to deliver a good final work product was hindered.

Failure to attain handwriting competency during the school-age years often has far-reaching negative effects on both academic success and self-esteem. Therefore, this guide is written in the hopes that parents and teachers will become familiar with the developmental components necessary to produce legible handwriting, activities to promote sound developmental skills, and how to spot simple versus more complex issues that require further evaluation.

Hoping you have a fun and informative ride,

Dr. Carol Leibovich-Mankes, DrOT, OTR/L, PLCC

Introduction
Handwriting Basics

The handwriting process is much like driving a car. Several components must be readily available to accomplish either of these activities. If one of these areas is not functioning efficiently, the goal cannot be successfully met.

	DRIVING	HANDWRITING
GOAL	**Reach a Destination**	**Legible Handwriting**
1st Requirement	**Sturdy Road—** Smooth Road	**Foundational Components—** NS, Sensory, Motor, Cognitive & Perceptual Systems
2nd Requirement	**Functioning Vehicle—** Brakes, Steering, Engine, Battery, etc.	**Performance Skills—** Strength/Endurance, Coordination, Hand Dominance, Hand Function, Motor Planning, Visual-Perceptual Oculomotor & Executive Functions
3rd Requirement	**Competent Driver—** Sit, Hold, & Steer the Wheel, & Familiarity with Driving Rules, which assist in reaching the destination (goal) safely	**· Task Execution—** Knowledge of Handwriting Rules, Sitting Posture, Pencil Grasp & Execute Handwriting Assignment

Good Focused Driver	**TASK EXECUTION** Execute & Follow Handwriting Rules

Well Functioning Vehicle	**PERFORMANCE SKILLS OF HANDWRITING** Strength/Endurance, Bilateral Coordination, Motor-Planning, Hand-Dominance, Hand Function, Fine Motor Skills, Visual-Motor Skills Visual-Perceptual, Oculomotor Skills & Executive Functions

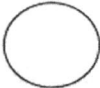 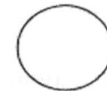

Sturdy Road	**FOUNDATIONAL COMPONENTS OF HANDWRITING** Building Blocks for Learning Motor, Cognitive, Sensory, Perceptual Systems

Section I
The Road-Foundational Components

The road is the foundation on which vehicles travel. If this foundation is not built well and made safe, the vehicle's ride will be bumpy, hindering the driving experience. The same philosophy is true with our body's systems. Our body's systems are the foundation, the first building block for learning. Well-functioning body systems facilitate the development of the learning process (e.g., handwriting, math, reading, etc.).

A system of roads is considered well maintained when it offers safety, road stability, and good driving conditions. Our body systems require similar components to function smoothly. The Nervous System provides the safety and smooth flow of information, the Musculoskeletal System provides the stability, and, finally, the Sensory, Cognitive,

Perceptual Systems, and Executive Functions provide us with the "good conditions," e.g., attention, memory, mental status, organization, and visual abilities enabling optimal learning and handwriting production.

Chapter 1
The Nervous System

The Nervous System can be described as a traffic-control center. It controls traffic in our body, maintaining safe and flawless functioning 24 hours a day. The Nervous System is composed of the Brain, Spinal Cord, and millions of Nerves.

The Brain—The Boss

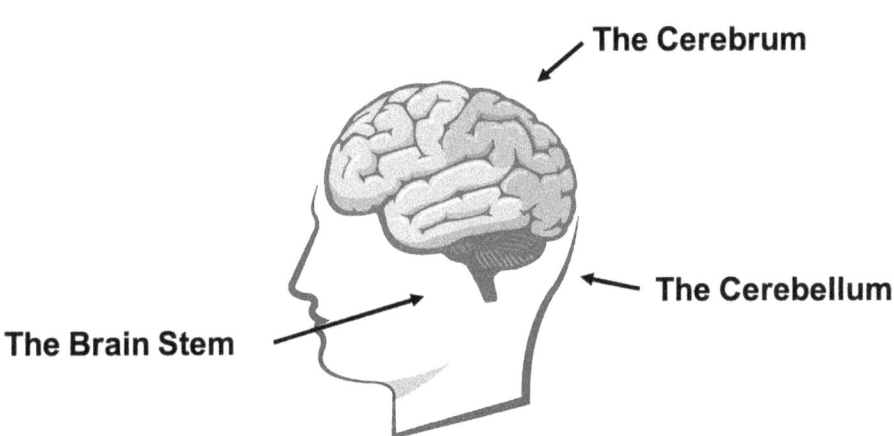

The Brain is protected by the skull. It is the boss of the control center. It has three parts: the Cerebrum, the Cerebellum, and the Brain Stem.

The Cerebrum

The Cerebrum, also known as the Cortex, is the largest part of the Brain. It contains two hemispheres that communicate with each other through a bundle of nerves. The left hemisphere controls the right side of the body, and the right hemisphere controls the left side of the body. The right side helps you think about abstract things like music, colors, and shapes. The left side is said to be more analytical, helping you with math, logic, and speech. These hemispheres are each further subdivided into four areas known as lobes. Each lobe has its own job description. The right and left hemispheres have a bridge between them that needs to have a sturdy connection. This bridge is known as the Corpus Coliseum, and it makes sure information between the two hemispheres runs smoothly and is well integrated.

The Cerebellum

The Cerebellum is in the back of the Brain. Its job is to maintain our balance and coordination, making them seem effortless.

The Brain Stem

The Brain Stem is located beneath the Cerebrum and in front of the Cerebellum. It connects the Brain to the Spinal Cord. The Brain Stem controls the involuntary functions of the body, the ones that keep us alive, such as breathing, digestion, and circulation of our blood.

The Spinal Cord—Highway

The Spinal Cord is a major highway. It carries sensory messages from the body to the Brain. It carries motor messages from the Brain back to all the muscles, organs, and glands in our body. These messages travel through electrical and chemical signals produced by our nerves.

The Nerves—Couriers

The Nerves are the Brain's helpers. Their job is to repeatedly network with other Nerves, thus making lasting connections. These connections become permanent, allowing us to accomplish everyday activities effortlessly. We each facilitate their job by practicing tasks on an ongoing basis (e.g., handwriting, bike riding, driving, etc.).

Chapter 2
The Sensory System

The Sensory System is the part of the nervous system responsible for processing sensory information. Sensory information includes information coming in from the outside world, such as vision, hearing, taste, touch, smell, vestibular functions (movement and balance). Sensory information is also the information that is solely felt within our body, such as pressure, temperature, and proprioception.

Information from our senses gets picked up by sensory nerves and then travels through our spinal cord to our brain. In the brain, the information is processed. A related response is sent through our motor nerves to produce an appropriate action. This process is known as sensory processing or sensory integration.

It is especially important to stimulate a child's five senses for the first 0–12 months of life, and thereafter at every age up to 6 years. This will assist the child in developing good sensory-processing abilities, which are responsible for the formation of healthy social interactions, motor skills, and attention for learning. However, just as a child can have a language delay, so can he/she have a developmentally-delayed sensory processing system.

A child who has a developmentally-delayed sensory-processing system will experience difficulties with processing information coming in through one or more of his/her five senses. A child may be too sensitive to information coming in from the senses; this is known as Hypersensitivity. A child may crave the information coming in from the senses; this is known as Hyposensitivity. Finally, a child might have a combination of both. Depending on the extent of the sensory concerns or effects on his/her functioning, the child may be diagnosed with Sensory Integration Dysfunction.

Sensory Integration Dysfunction translates into an immature, disorganized nervous system. The child's brain gets overwhelmed by incoming sensory input, creating a "traffic jam," which leads to a "fight-or-flight" feeling of anxiety and frustration. This feeling of loss of control also diminishes the child's ability to pay attention and learn.

Vision-Visual Sense

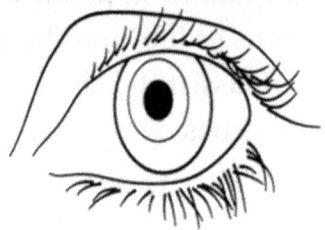

The Visual System consists of two functional parts, the Eye and part of the Brain. The eye detects and focuses on "something in the environment," just like a camera. It allows us to see. The brain does all the complex image processing, allowing us to make sense of what we see. For example, a baby sees a shiny object, and then the brain processes it as what the object is—a flashlight or a mirror, etc. Vision is a fundamental factor in the learning process. The four interrelated areas of visual function are: Visual-Perception, Visual-Motor, Visual-Acuity, and Oculomotor skills.

Signs of an Inefficient Visual-Processing System

Over-Responsive Child Hypersensitive	Under-Responsive Child Hyposensitive
• Appears irritated by sunlight or bright lights • Is easily distracted by visual stimuli • Avoids eye contact • May become overstimulated in brightly colored rooms	• Has difficulty controlling eye movements and tracking objects • Mixes up similar letters • Focuses on little details in a picture and misses the whole • Loses his/her place frequently when reading or copying from the blackboard

Treatment Strategies & Tools

- Simplify worksheets and make them less visually cluttered.
- Use diagrams to organize information on paper.
- Use a slanted board (or three-ring binder) to bring the work closer to the child's field of vision.
- Use highlighters to highlight information while reading.
- Use verbal cues to clarify assignments and directions.
- Use graph paper for math problems.
- Control lighting in the room.
- Use sunglasses when outside.
- Use index cards to block out other sections of a worksheet or lines of text while reading.
- Provide opportunities for games involving hidden pictures or looking for items (e.g., I Spy).
- Provide games requiring attending to details, such as "what's different/same."
- Allow extended time to complete work.
- Give breaks to avoid overwhelming or fatiguing the visual system.

Hearing-Auditory Sense

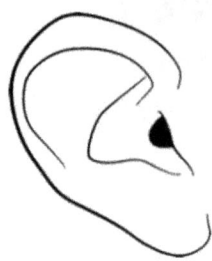

The sensory organ of the Auditory System is the Ear. Vibrations in the air reach the ear and are then sent to the brain, where they are converted into meaningful sounds.

Signs of an Inefficient Auditory Processing System

Over-Responsive Child Hypersensitive	Under-Responsive Child Hyposensitive
• Covers his/her ears • Is distracted by sounds • Does not notice others • Fears toilets flushing, hairdryers, and/or vacuums • Resists going to loud public places (even cafeteria at school)	• May not respond to verbal cues • Craves loud music and making noise • May appear confused about where a sound is coming from and/or may say, "What?" frequently

Treatment Strategies & Tools

- Arrange for the child to sit in front of class, in front of teacher.

- Use FM system to minimize distractions and so that oral information comes in as clearly as possible.

- Provide visual cues, along with oral instruction, to facilitate understanding.

- Use headphones or white noise to buffer background environmental auditory distractions.

- Use slower speech and different tones to accentuate important information.

- Use key words to indicate what's coming and what's important, in order to minimize the possibility that the child will miss information or steps.

- Provide opportunity for music and experiment with different sound frequencies.

Touch-Tactile Sense

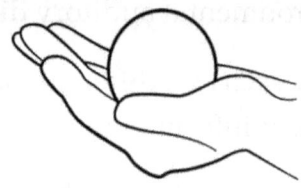

Touch is also known as the Tactile System. The Tactile System is the first to develop in infancy. This system involves Nerves located under the skin. These Nerves provide a person with information about light touch, outside temperature, and pressure. Processing this information effectively allows us to feel safe, which in turn allows us to bond with those who love us and to develop socially and emotionally.

The Tactile System is composed of two separate systems: Discriminative and Protective.

Discriminative System: This allows us to determine where we are being touched and what is touching us.

Protective System: This tells us when we are in contact with something dangerous. It causes a flight, fright, or fight response.

Signs of an Inefficient Tactile-Processing System

Over-Responsive Child Hypersensitive	Under-Responsive Child Hyposensitive
• May refuse or resist messy play • Resists cuddling, kisses, and light touch • Dislikes rough clothes or seams in socks • Resists baths, showers, or going to the beach	• May not realize hands or face are dirty • Touches everything and anything constantly • May be self-abusive, play rough with peers, and/or may not feel pain (may even enjoy it!)

Treatment Strategies & Tools

- Provide advance warning when approaching or wanting to hug, kiss, or pat, e.g., "I'm going to give you a bath, so I'll drizzle a drop of water on you first."

- Provide opportunities for heavy work, firm-pressure exercises, and fidgets to reorganize the sensory system, e.g., vacuuming, riding a bike, pushing a shopping cart, carrying groceries, and even climbing playground equipment.

- Warn or provide extra cues for possibly dangerous situations.

- Give choice of fabric and foods to minimize anxiety related to different textures.

Taste-Gustatory Smell-Olfactory Senses

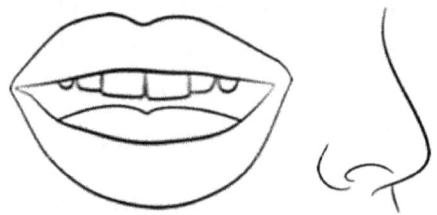

The major sense organ of the Olfactory System is the Nose and of the Gustatory System is the Mouth. The senses of smell and taste are usually considered together because they affect each other's experience.

Over-Responsive Child Hypersensitive	Under-Responsive Child Hyposensitive
• May be overly bothered by certain smells • Chooses foods based on smell	• May not notice unpleasant smells

Treatment Strategies & Tool

- Be aware of what smells irritate or calm your child down.

- Have available a tool kit that contains items to calm your child, e.g., soothing smells to counteract smells your child finds unpleasant, nose plugs, air purifiers, etc.

- Keep vents circulating in the car.

Signs of an Inefficient Gustatory-Processing System

Over-Responsive Child Hypersensitive	Under-Responsive Child Hyposensitive
• May be a picky eater • May gag on textured food • May dislike brushing his/her teeth	• May lick and put inedible objects in his/her mouth • Chews on pencils, shirts, etc.

Treatment Strategies & Tools

- Provide chewy toys or crunchy food for mouth, e.g., pretzels, apples, Chewy Tubes, gum.

- Use a vibrating toothbrush.

- Allow to use sports water bottle or have smoothies during the day, using a straw.

- Play games during the day, e.g., blow bubbles, whistle, blow up balloons.

Body Awareness—Proprioception

Proprioception is the internal sense that tells you where your body parts are without your having to look at them. This information is given to us through our Joints and Muscles.

Information about body position travels through the spinal cord and into parts of the brain, allowing us to move and balance our bodies without having to think about it.

Signs of an Inefficient Proprioceptive-Processing System

Over-Responsive Child Hypersensitive	Under-Responsive Child Hyposensitive
• Constantly jumping, crashing, and stomping • Loves to be squished and given bear hugs • Prefers tight clothing • Loves roughhousing • May be aggressive with other children	• Has difficulty understanding where body is in relation to other objects • Appears clumsy, bumps into things often • Moves in a stiff and/or uncoordinated way

A child who has difficulty regulating this type of input may not know how hard to push on an object and may misjudge the weight of an object, break objects often, and rip his/her paper when erasing pencil marks. During handwriting tasks, the child may either exert not enough or too much pressure on the pencil or eraser.

Treatment Strategies & Tools

- Play games that teach directionality (up/down/right/left), e.g., obstacle course, Simon Says, etc.

- Provide opportunity for movement and heavy work, e.g., marching, animal walks, and jumping/crashing on the bed.

- Increase input to hands by using clay, Play-Doh, cutting thick paper, exploration of various textures.

- Encourage participation in sports, e.g., swimming, martial arts, gymnastics, playground activities.

- When showing too little pressure on writing tool, allow child to use a ballpoint pen or marker, try a weighted pencil, or use carbon paper to challenge student to increase pressure.

Movement-Vestibular Sense

The Vestibular Sense is our sense of movement and gravity, which originates from the Inner Ear. It gives the awareness of position and movement of the head. It lets a person know if their head is upright or tilted (even with eyes closed). The Vestibular System helps integrate all the other senses and brings about their balance. The Vestibular Sense contributes to attention, stable vision, verbal comprehension, and speech.

Signs of an Inefficient Vestibular-Processing System

Over-Responsive Child Hypersensitive	Under-Responsive Child Hyposensitive
• Avoids playground and moving equipment • Is fearful of heights, dislikes being tipped upside down • Is often afraid of falling, walking on uneven surfaces • Avoids rapid, sudden, or rotating movements	• Craves any possible movement experience, especially those that are fast or spinning • Never seems to sit still, shakes leg while sitting • Is a thrill seeker, loves being tossed in the air • Never seems to get dizzy • Is full of excess energy

Treatment Strategies & Tools

- Provide opportunity for movement, e.g., trampoline, swing, slide, spin, hang upside down, dance, balance, therapy ball for bouncing, rocking chair, scooter board.

- Be aware that movement can be overstimulating for some children, so learn the signs and follow movement with heavy work, such as push-ups, tug-of-war, wheelbarrow walking, etc.

Chapter 3
The Musculoskeletal System

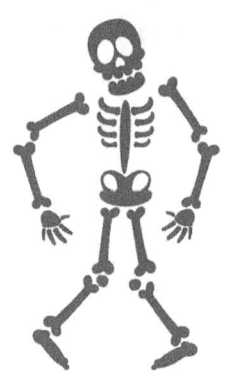

The Musculoskeletal System supports and protects our body and gives us the ability to move. Its proper functioning depends on an efficient Nervous System and the integrity of the Bones, Muscles, and Ligaments. Without these body parts, you and your child wouldn't be able to stand, walk, run, or even sit.

Bones

The 206 Bones in our body make up the skeleton, which helps transmit movement throughout our body. The Bones vary in size and shape.

Muscles

The movements your Muscles make are coordinated and controlled by the Brain and Nervous System. Movement is a result of messages sent through Motor Nerves, telling Muscles to contract. Muscles generally work in pairs to produce movement. When one Muscle flexes (i.e., contracts), the other relaxes. Each Muscle has its own special name and function. However, Muscles generally are described as Involuntary or Voluntary.

Involuntary Muscles are also known as Smooth Muscles. They're controlled by the Nervous System, specifically the Brain Stem. A person does not have to try to make these Muscles move; they just do automatically.

Voluntary Muscles are controlled by us. When we want to move an arm, leg, or neck, sensory messages are sent to the Brain (Cerebral Motor Cortex and Cerebellum), and responses are sent back through a Motor Nerve, telling our Muscles to move.

Strength & Endurance

Strength is being able to use muscles against some form of resistance. Endurance is being able to do an activity for longer periods of time. Endurance activities involve continuous movement. They benefit the heart, lungs, and circulatory system.

Core & Upper Extremity Stability

Muscles in the Trunk, Shoulder, and Wrist work together to provide us with joint stability. When writing, we rely on our trunk to provide proper, strong, and stable posture, and to allow us to sit up straight and execute controlled movement of our arms. If these muscles are not stable and strong, our pencil control will be flimsy when writing.

Chapter 4
Cognitive & Perceptual System

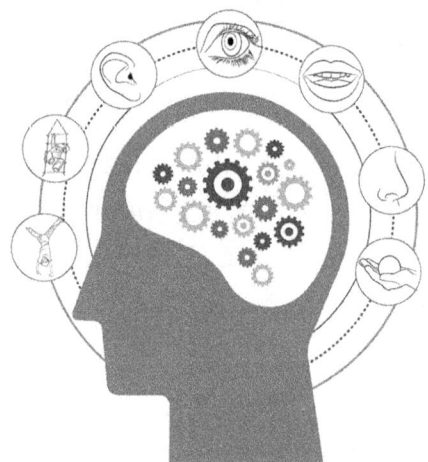

Cognitive Component

Cognitive Processing is a post-sensory function of the Brain. Immediately after sensory information comes in, the cognitive system sets about interpreting and organizing the sensory input into meaningful information. Cognitive abilities include problem solving, attention, perception, memory, and language.

By the end of 3 years (36 months), your child:

- Makes mechanical toys work.
- Matches an object in his/her hand or room to a picture in a book.

- Plays make-believe with dolls, animals, and people.
- Sorts objects by shape and color.
- Completes puzzles with three or four pieces.
- Understands concept of "two".

By the end of 4 years (48 months), your child:

- Correctly names some colors.
- Understands the concept of counting and may know a few numbers.
- Tries to solve problems from a single point of view.
- Begins to have a clearer sense of time.
- Follows three-part commands.
- Recalls parts of a story.
- Understands the concepts of "same" and "different".
- Engages in fantasy play.

By the end of 5 years (60 months), your child:

- Counts 10 or more objects.
- Correctly names at least four colors.
- Better understands the concept of time.
- Knows about things used every day in the home (appliances, food).

Perceptual Component

Perception is the Cognitive Process of understanding what we are looking at. This is done by our Brain. It transforms sensory information related to hearing, taste, smell, vision, touch proprioception, and motion into information about the events, objects, or people around us (e.g., size, distance, texture, etc.). Handwriting has many perceptual requirements, such as letter direction, size, form, and spacing. Poor perception can make production of legible print very difficult.

Section II
The Vehicle-Performance Skills

A vehicle must have certain characteristics that ensure the vehicle will be able to perform well while driving under various conditions. Some examples are balanced tires, an engine that runs, fuel, etc. A person's body works much the same way. In a person, these characteristics are known as performance skills.

Performance skills are the vehicle by which a person executes daily tasks. These skills are learned, and they enable a person to carry out a task with minimum energy and time. Performance skills develop in a healthy manner only if the foundational components are well established and work as a team to guide performance skills. Execution of performance skills requires our brains to coordinate sensory input from the five senses (sight, sound, taste, touch, and smell) with the proprioceptive and vestibular senses, which work on an unconscious level. These send the appropriate signals to the body's muscles, thus producing the appropriate action.

Handwriting is one important academic task that can be greatly affected if these foundational systems and performance skills are not working at an optimal level. Quality of handwriting is affected by several performance skills. These include trunk control, balance, shoulder stability, endurance, gross-motor skills, motor planning, bilateral integration, crossing midline, eye-hand coordination, fine-motor skills, and established hand dominance.

Chapter 1
Gross-Motor Skills

Gross-Motor Skills are movements related to the large-muscle groups (trunk, arms, legs), such as running and jumping.

Gross-Motor Skill Milestones

0-1 years: Control head, roll, sit, crawl, and walk

1-2 years: Walk, run, and throw

2-3 years: Jump, kick, throw, and catch

3-4 years: Ride tricycle, hop, jump, and play on jungle gym

4-5 years: Do one-leg stand, climb, heel-toe walk, do somersaults, swim, dance, and ballet

5-6 years: Exhibit advanced balance, walk on toes, catch one-handed, dribble ball, and skip rhythmically

Developments Needed for a Child to Progress through Milestones

- Overall strength and endurance.
- Bilateral coordination and midline crossing.
- Motor planning.

1. Overall Strength/Endurance

Strength is the force/pressure a body's muscles exhibit when producing an action, e.g., holding a tennis racket or a pencil, cutting with scissors or fork and knife, etc. Endurance is the ability to do something repeatedly and not get tired easily, e.g., running, walking, sitting, swimming, writing, etc.

Treatment Strategies & Tools

- Doing sit-ups and push-ups, crossing monkey bars, climbing trees, or even building snowmen—these all strengthen muscles.

- Helping parents carry in groceries and doing household chores and yard work also help children become stronger.

How Do Strength and Endurance Impact Handwriting?

Having overall Strength and Endurance allows the child to sustain posture for the required time to complete the written work. For example, note-taking in 3rd grade requires a greater amount of strength and endurance than in 1st grade due to the quantity of written work. If a child did not develop sufficient overall strength and endurance, he/she would exert so much energy trying to keep his/her body upright that it would negatively affect his/her level of writing. He/she may feel fatigued quickly; therefore, his/her writing and handwriting quality may not reflect his/her full academic potential.

2. Bilateral Integration & Crossing Midline

Bilateral Integration and Crossing Midline work as a team. They give us the ability to use both sides of the body in a coordinated manner, facilitating daily tasks, such as handwriting.

Bilateral Integration refers to the child's ability to use both sides of his or her body in an activity. This is accomplished by participating in activities that strengthen the connection between the right and left hemispheres of the brain. Bilateral Integration develops through stages.

Stages of Bilateral Integration

a. Symmetrical Bilateral Integration

This occurs when both sides of the body perform the same movement at the same time (mirror image). An example is when a baby starts playing with his/her hands and/or feet together at the same time. At this point, the baby's brain learns that both hands must work together for the play to happen. Older children practice this stage by jumping with both feet together, clapping hands, and pumping their legs to move themselves backwards and forwards on a swing.

b. Reciprocal Bilateral Integration

At this stage, the child starts moving one side of the body in a reciprocal manner to the other side of the body. Crawling is the most basic form of Reciprocal Bilateral Integration. Walking up and down stairs one foot at a time, marching, skipping, and climbing a ladder are examples of daily activities which further refine this stage of bilateral integration.

c. Asymmetrical Bilateral Integration

This is a critical time in the child's Bilateral Integration Development. If this stage is not reinforced, its poor development strongly hinders the success of the next two stages. Asymmetrical Bilateral Integration takes place when each side of the body learns to perform a different action, but the actions of both sides of the body are needed in order to complete the task. This is trickier than the previous stages because the brain now must work out how to time two different actions simultaneously. Dancing, eating with a knife and fork, and even getting dressed are all daily instances in which we use Asymmetrical Bilateral Integration. A child can enhance this form of Bilateral Integration by playing ball games (kicking and throwing), threading beads, cutting out pictures, buttoning something, and tying laces. Fun ways to reinforce Asymmetrical Bilateral Integration are dancing sequences (e.g., "step together, step, hop") and musical exercises (e.g., banging on a drum).

d. Crossing Midline

This occurs at about age 4. The body is now ready to cross the arms or legs over its midline. The midline is an imaginary line that runs through the body, cutting it in half from head to toe. Examples of Crossing Midline include babies banging two blocks together or a preschooler holding scissors with one hand while manipulating the paper with the other.

e. Hand Dominance

This is the highest form of Bilateral Integration. It is an indication that connections between the right and left hemispheres of the brain were solidified. The more developed a child's Bilateral Integration, the greater his/her chance of developing a consistent dominant hand, whether left or right.

Hand Dominance refers to the hand you use for daily tasks, such as writing and eating. Most people are right-hand dominant, some are left, and others are ambidextrous, i.e., they use either hand. While handwriting, a child would use his/her dominant hand to write and his/her nondominant hand to stabilize the paper.

Children with poor Bilateral Integration and Midline Crossing tend to use the hand closest to the object to pick it up, even though it may not be their dominant hand. As a result, the nondominant hand may be performing tasks other than practicing its job of stabilizing an object. Also, this situation robs the dominant hand of those opportunities to develop, practice, and refine its skills.

The myth that there could be something wrong with your child if he/she is left-handed should be put to rest. A child with a dominant left hand should never be forced to become right-handed. It is more common for left-handed children and adults to swap hands for different tasks. This is normal if it is consistent, i.e., always throwing a ball with the right hand, but always writing with the left hand.

How Do Bilateral Coordination/Midline Crossing /Hand Dominance Impact Handwriting?

If these components are not fully developed, the child will have a difficult time switching hands during an activity or using both hands efficiently together while tying shoes, cutting, drawing, and holding the book page open while writing with the other hand. The child will tend to use both hands equally, not allowing one hand to be refined to the extent that, for example, manipulation of the writing utensil is as efficient as possible. This will both decrease the quality of the handwriting and slow down the progress of the handwritten work. It will be harder for the child to visually track from left to right, or right to left, and therefore more difficult to read and copy from a book or board, all of which are activities that are often done while handwriting.

Signs of Difficulty with Bilateral Coordination /Midline Crossing/Hand Dominance

- Switching hands in the middle of coloring and/or handwriting.

- Using left hand for activities on the left side of the body and right hand for activities on the right side, instead of crossing over.

- Demonstrating difficulty with reading, handwriting, and overall coordination of gross-motor patterns (crawling, skipping, jumping jacks).

Treatment Strategies & Tools

- Encourage your child to practice activities that build Bilateral Integration skills, using both sides of the body, separately and together.
    - Jumping and skipping.
    - Riding a bike.
    - Catching a ball.

- Beating a drum.
- Buttoning.
- Tying laces.
- Threading beads.
- Cutting with scissors.
- Provide opportunities for Midline Crossing in everyday activities, e.g., place objects on the other side of the child's body so they are forced to cross the midline when picking them up.
- Play games, e.g., bring left elbow to your right knee, crawling games, etc.

3. Motor Planning

Motor Planning, also known as Praxis, refers to a child's ability to figure out how to perform a new motor task. For a child to produce an action, he/she must first understand the task, then plan how to perform the task, and finally carry out the task. However, if the connections between the brain and the body are not working well, an appropriate motor action will not occur. Before we can produce any new movements, the brain must organize all the environmental information coming in through our senses. Then, the brain sends signals to our muscles, letting them know at what speed, force, and timing we should move.

Motor skills are movements carried out by the body when the brain, nervous system, and muscles work together. Therefore, if one of these systems malfunctions or is not well developed, a child will experience difficulties with his motor skills. Motor-skills development progresses from gross- to fine-motor skills. A child must have well-developed gross-motor skills to enable the development of good fine-motor skills.

How Does Motor Planning Impact Handwriting?

Motor Planning plays an important part in handwriting. It plays a role in stabilizing and moving the pencil while writing and in producing an efficient pencil grasp. It also enables the child to accurately reproduce the required letter shapes. The child needs to think of the letter or word that he/she needs to produce and get his/her body to execute the motor actions necessary to produce what he/she wants on paper.

Treatment Strategies & Tools

- Provide the child an opportunity to practice, practice, and practice different movement patterns and forming letters and words, until movements and handwriting become automatic. Automatic is defined as doing things without having to think much about how you are doing them. For example, driving, getting your car from point A to point B without having to continuously think of all the steps the task requires.
- Make handwriting practice fun by using shaving cream, rice buckets, art projects, etc.
- Enroll children in structured sports, e.g., dance, swimming, martial arts, gymnastics, tennis, etc.
- Draw and trace a large, sideways figure eight on the sidewalk or a dry board.

Chapter 2
Good Posture

Good Posture is the ability of the child to stay upright against gravity while changing body positions. If the child must concentrate on keeping himself/herself upright, his/her performance will be affected. He/she will be focused on sitting up in the chair, not on completing his/her writing task. Good Posture requires several components.

1. Trunk Control/Balance

Large muscles in the trunk must have good and balanced strength. The back and stomach muscles must keep us balanced while we move in any direction. Trunk stability is an important component for carrying out tasks that require a person to sit upright.

2. Shoulder Stability

The shoulder is the joint at the point where the arm attaches to the body. Shoulder stability develops when an infant props on the elbows while lying on his/her stomach.

How Does Posture Impact Handwriting?

If our trunk cannot keep us upright, we will not be able to produce accurate movements, thus compromising the quality of handwriting. Our handwriting would be illegible. Having shoulder stability means having the strength to keep your upper arms steady and against your body so that you can use your hands to complete a task. If these joints are not stable, the fine-motor control needed for writing is impossible to achieve.

Treatment Strategies & Tools

- Provide your child with opportunities to strengthen his/her trunk, shoulders, elbows, and wrists, e.g., wheelbarrow walking, animal walks, modified push-ups, sit-ups, therapy-ball sitting, balance-beam walking, etc.

- Practice fine-motor activities, such as coloring and writing on a vertical surface. Tape the paper on a wall or use an easel.

- Practice fine-motor activities, such as puzzles, coloring, and writing, while your child is lying on the floor and propped on his/her elbows.

This exercise is an enjoyable way to improve coordination and upper-arm strength.

Instructions: Tell one child (A) to lie on the ground with his hands flat on the floor in front of him. His partner (B) should then take hold of A's feet. Have A straighten his arms and push his body off the floor so he can walk on his hands. B should then steer A around the room, holding his feet like the handles of a wheelbarrow. After going round the room once, have the partners switch places.

Chapter 3
Fine-Motor Skills

Fine-motor skills are movements carried out by small-muscle groups (fingers, toes, wrists, lips, and tongue) when completing activities such as feeding, dressing, drawing, writing, and cutting. Weak fine-motor skills are related to a child's struggle with handwriting.

Fine-Motor Development Milestones

0-1 years: Grasp (close/open active hands).

1-2 years: Manipulate small objects, grasp, release. Build towers and puzzles.

2-3 years: Screw lids, grasp crayons, trace verticals, put shoes on.

3-4 years: Draw, use eye-hand coordination, cut with scissors.

4-5 years: Use mature pencil grip, draw, put toothpaste on toothbrush.

5-6 years: Thread/tie shoelaces, draw, cut, write letters/figures/short words.

Skills Needed to Progress through these Milestones

1. Hand Strength & Endurance

Children should have strength, endurance, and dexterity in their wrists, hands, and fingers before being asked to manipulate a pencil on paper. Working on strength and dexterity first can eliminate the development of an inappropriate pencil grasp, which is becoming more commonplace as young children are engaged in writing experiences before their hands are ready.

2. *Grasp Development*

Grasp development starts as a primitive reflex (power grip) and develops into a voluntary, more precise prehension (index-finger/thumb opposition). This is also the typical progression of handwriting grasp development. A few children will jump stages, while others go through a phase of using a combination of grasps. This is good because they figure out for themselves which grasp works best for their hands.

Progression of Grasp Development

Palmar Supinate (12-18 months)

Distal Pronate (24-36 months)

Static Tripod (3.6- 4 years)

Dynamic Tripod (4.6 - 6 years)

(Erhardt, 1982)

Examples of a child using a Palmar, Distal Pronate, Static Grasp, and unestablished hand dominance:

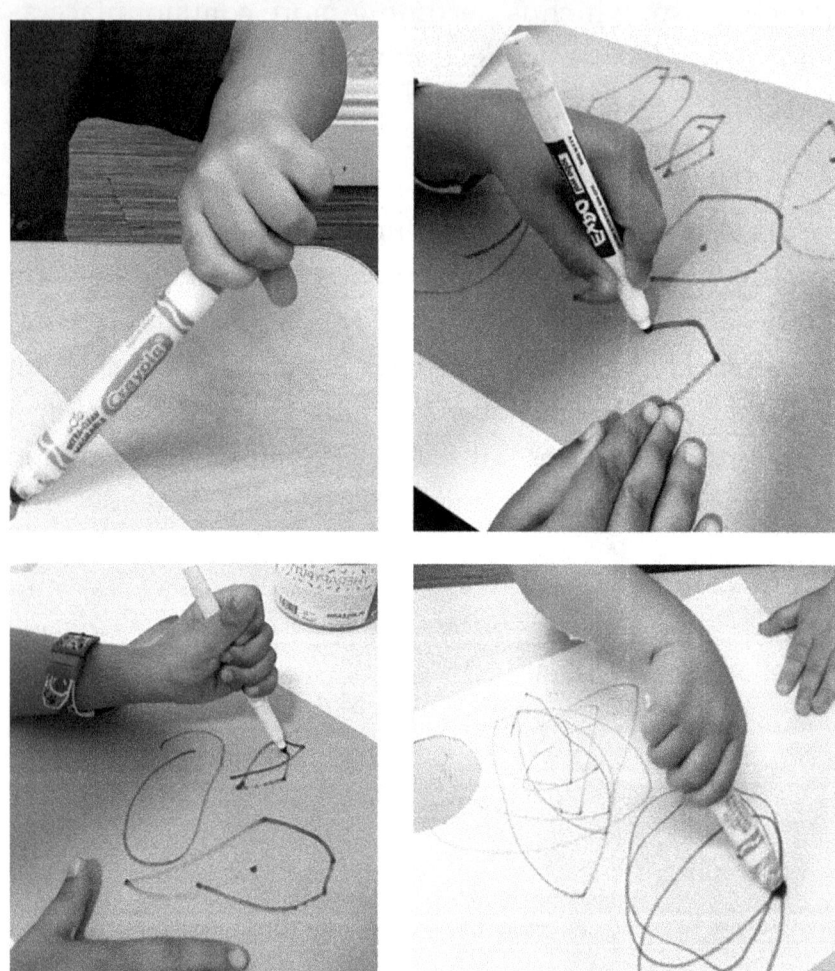

Components of Grasp Development

a. Palmar Arches

Palmar arches are arches which shape the hand, enabling the grasping of different objects. These arches also allow for manipulation of small objects by the fingers and determine the power of the grip.

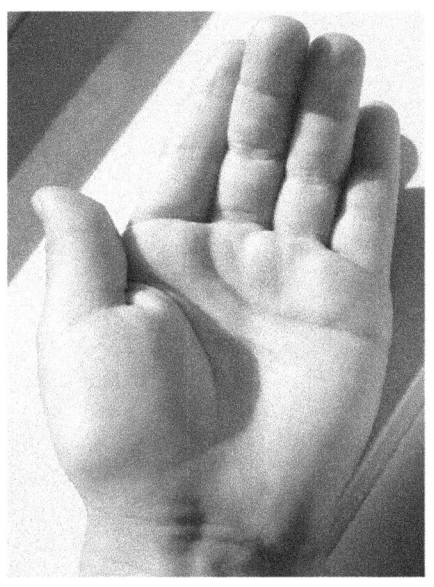

b. Thumb Opposition and Opening Web Space

To develop a good pencil grip, a child must have stability and strength in the muscles of the wrist, fingers, thumb, and the base of the thumb. This enables the maintenance of an open web space while holding a pencil.

c. In-Hand Manipulation

Picking up an item and being able to move it around in your hand, e.g., coins, beads, etc.

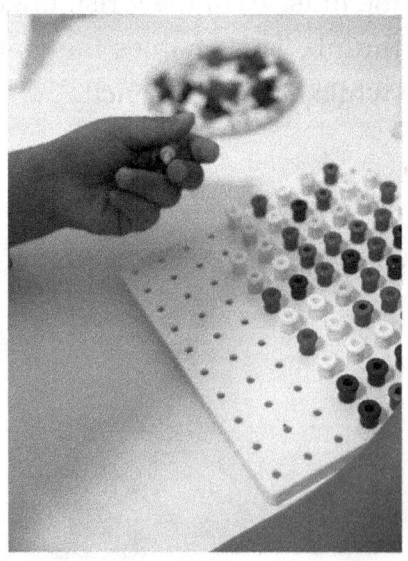

3. Scissor Grasp

When scissors are held correctly and they fit a child's hand well, cutting activities will exercise the very same muscles that are needed to manipulate a pencil in a mature tripod grasp. The correct scissor position is with the dominant hand's thumb placed in the smaller handle, the last three fingers (starting with the middle finger) placed through the larger handle and the index finger on the outside of the handle to stabilize.

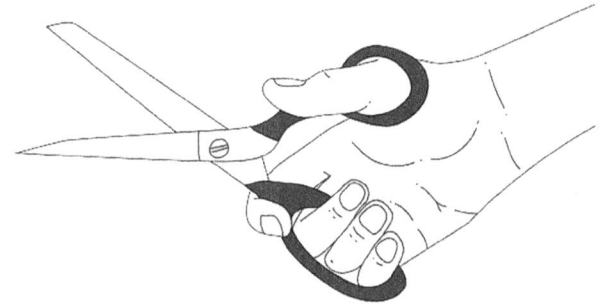

How Do Fine-Motor Skills Impact Handwriting?

They affect handwriting legibility and speed due to decreased pencil control.

Children with decreased fine-motor skills are shown to need more time to complete writing activities, they drop items more frequently, and they have more difficulty completing other self-care activities, such as dressing, eating, etc.

Treatment Strategies & Tools

- Play with Play-Doh. Use a rolling pin to tool the Play-Doh. Use index finger and thumb to roll it into small balls and/or roll "snakes" and then cut it with scissors.

- Use handheld hole punch to make holes in paper.
- String beads, cereal, or macaroni, use tweezers, and do art projects in which child needs to use pincer grasp (index and thumb) to pick up small objects.
- Tear paper into small pieces, crumple, and glue.
- Pick up cotton balls using spring-loaded clothespins.
- Use spray bottle to spray plants or clean a desk.
- Use pencil grip to encourage proper use of intrinsic muscles of the hands.
- Place 10–20 pennies, beads, or beans on a table. Pick them up with index finger and thumb only and then move them to palm of same hand.
- Play with puzzles, LEGOs, building blocks, battleship toys, spin tops, etc.
- Encourage child to start and end activity with same hand in order to develop dominant-hand dexterity, strength, and endurance.
- Have child make an okay sign and then proceed to touch each finger to the thumb individually.
- Use hands as much as possible and practice, practice, practice!!!

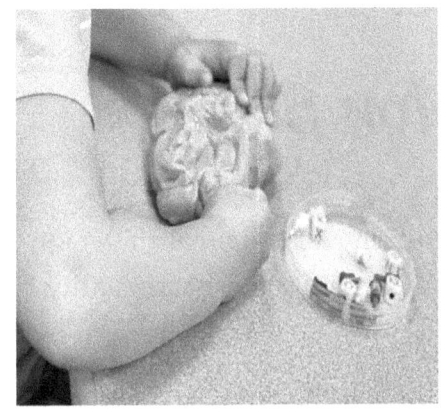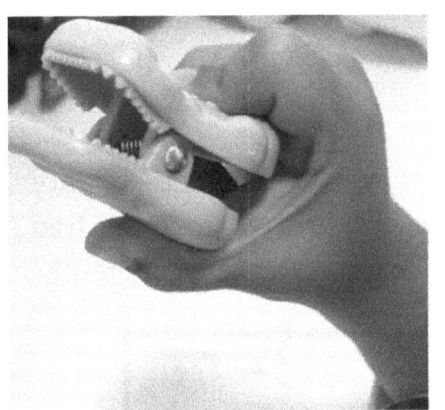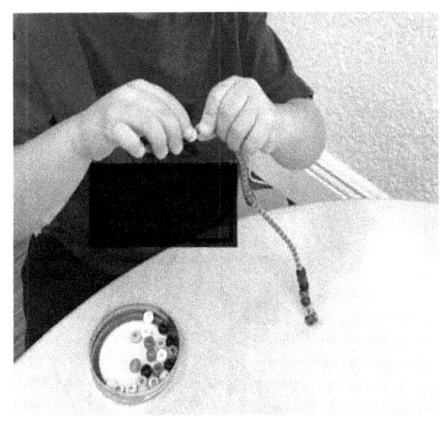

Chapter 4
Visual-Motor Skills

As mentioned previously, the four interrelated areas of visual function are: Visual-Motor, Visual-Perception, Visual-Acuity, and Oculomotor skills.

Visual-Motor Skills are a child's ability to draw and/or copy what he/she sees, e.g., shapes, letters, or numbers. It is the process that links what the eye sees to what the hand produces.

Below are approximations of the developmental sequence for drawing strokes. These will vary greatly since children develop at different rates and are exposed to tasks differently.

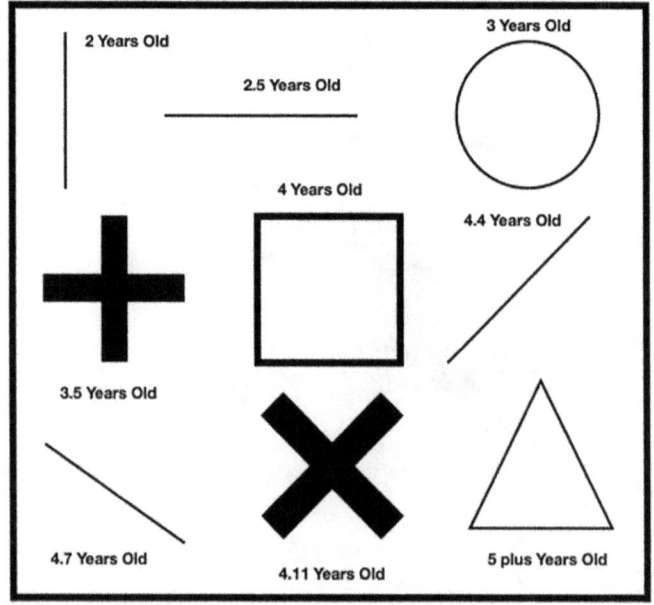

How Do Visual-Motor Skills Impact Handwriting?

Weak Visual-Motor Skills make it more difficult for a child to accurately copy shapes, write, etc. For example, a child may struggle with producing a letter, number, or shape without it appearing disjointed or wavy. Handwriting may seem to take up much more energy than it should, the energy expended out of proportion to the task.

REMEMBER: Visual-Motor Skills, such as copying, may also be negatively affected by weak Visual-Perceptual, Fine-Motor, and Eye Coordination Skills.

Treatment Strategies & Tools

- Trace and use stencils to draw shapes.
- Complete mazes.
- Play Tic-Tac-Toe (good practice for circles and diagonal lines).
- Color (encourage children over age 4 to color inside the lines).
- Play Connect the Dots.
- Draw half a shape, and let child complete the other half.
- String beads and create/follow a pattern.
- Practice with Lacing Cards.
- Make shapes with sticks.
- Draw with chalk on sidewalk or blackboard.

- Draw shapes with highlighter, and let child trace over.
- Practice drawing different pictures using templates, e.g., art books or Internet.
- Practice, practice, practice!!!

Chapter 5
Visual-Perceptual Skills

The second interrelated area of visual function is Visual Perception.

Visual-Perceptual Skills help children understand visual information coming in from the environment. Visual-Perceptual Skills play an important role in handwriting. These skills are important for forming, copying, sizing, spacing, and orienting letters and words correctly. These skills have several components.

1. **Form Constancy** is the ability to identify a form even if it is different in size, orientation, color, or texture. A child with good Visual Form-Constancy skills will recognize an object, word, letter, or number, no matter how it is presented. A child with Poor Form Constancy will have a difficult time learning to read and write. He/she may frequently reverse letters and numbers.

2. **Figure Ground** is the ability to distinguish a form from the surrounding background. A child with Poor Figure Ground will have a hard time identifying a particular word in a paragraph, drawing a straight line between boundaries, copying from the blackboard or textbook without constantly losing his/her place, and/or

finding objects, such as his/her socks in a drawer with other clothes. This child may also seem inattentive, disorganized, and unable to keep his/her place while reading or doing math work.

3. **Spatial Relations/Position** in Space is the ability to understand the position of objects in relation to one's own body. A child experiencing Poor Spatial Relations may find it difficult to put letters in the proper sequence while reading or spelling. He/she may also be unable to remember the sequence involved in solving problems, be unable to read a map, have difficulty organizing thoughts into sentences, and have poor spacing between letters while writing.

4. **Visual Discrimination** is the ability to tell the differences and similarities between forms. A child with Poor Visual-Discrimination skills has a difficult time recognizing that "was" and "saw" are different words, even though they have the same letters, and gets confused by similar shapes and letters.

5. **Visual Closure** is the ability to identify a form even though part of it is not visible. Poor Visual Closure does not allow a child to complete and/or identify a drawing or letter if given only a part of it, for example, if the quality of a photocopy is poor.

6. **Visual Memory** is the ability to remember what one sees. A child with Poor Visual-Memory may have difficulty remembering the alphabet,

learning basic math facts, reading, and spelling. He/she may also be slow in copying from the blackboard and be unable to remember the sequence of events, story, numbers, and letters.

7. **Directionality** is the knowledge of right and left on one's own body. A child with Poor Directionality may have a hard time understanding, e.g., in, out, over, above, below, through, left, and right. He/she may also show letter and number reversals.

How Do Visual-Perceptual Skills Impact Handwriting?

Poor Visual-Perceptual Skills have a negative impact on letter and number recall, formation and directionality, legibility (space, size, and alignment), and organization of the written work.

Treatment Strategies & Tools

- Use color-coded handwriting paper showing top and bottom line.
- Use graph paper for math.
- Make sure worksheet copies are clear and maximize visibility.
- Reduce visual clutter on desk, board, etc.
- Use different colors to highlight important information.

- Break down visual assignments into small chunks.

- Use multisensory modalities to introduce material.

- Play games to reinforce visual-perceptual skills, such as Hidden Pictures, I Spy, puzzles, Same or Different, memory games, etc.

Chapter 6
Visual-Acuity & Oculomotor Function

Finally, the third and fourth interrelated areas of visual function are Visual Acuity and Oculomotor Function.

Visual Acuity, also known as Accommodation, refers to eyesight. This is the ability to focus near or far by controlling the shape of the lens inside the eye. The ability to see clearly at a far distance, such as 20 feet, and the ability to see clearly at a near distance, such as 16 inches, is considered optimum.

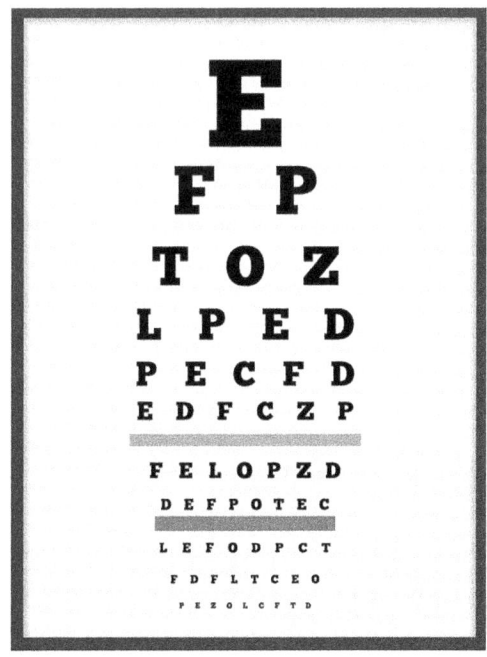

Oculomotor-Function Skills let us accurately direct our eye movements. Good Oculomotor-Function Skills require strong and coordinated muscles of the eye. The eye should be able to follow a line of print without losing its place. It should also be able to work with the other eye, allowing information retained by both eyes to form a single image.

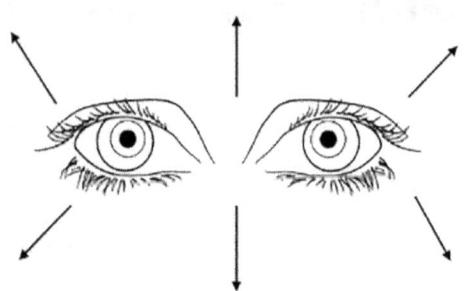

How Do Oculomotor Skills Impact Handwriting?

Well-developed Oculomotor Skills are important for sports, e.g., catching, hitting, or kicking a moving ball.

These skills are also important for schoolwork. In reading, the eyes must move left to right along a straight line. If a child cannot control these eye movements, he/she will lose his/her place, and comprehension then becomes a problem.

In handwriting, a child may poorly space and misalign letters or numbers. He/she may show persistent reversing of numbers, letters, or words after 2nd grade.

Treatment Strategies & Tools

- Provide child with a desktop model of information to be copied and/or seat student closer to board.

- Provide notes in an outline format in order to minimize copying/writing.

- Do activities, such as bubble blowing, balloon volleyball, tennis, Ping-Pong, and any other game in which you must keep your eyes on a moving target.

- Practice skills, such as scanning, using worksheet mazes, Word Search, and/or Find the Difference.

Chapter 7
Executive Functions

How Does Executive Function Impact Handwriting?

Executive Function is the ability to get things done. When a child needs to handwrite a word, sentence, or paragraph, he/she needs to attend, process, remember, initiate, organize, and perform. He/she must then check for errors; if any are found, they must be corrected. If a child has weak Executive Function, the task of writing a simple sentence may prove exhausting, and the result will be sloppy handwriting.

Possible Signs & Symptoms of Executive-Function Deficits

- Refuses to do homework—May have difficulty with initiation.

- Forgets or loses materials—May have difficulty with organization.

- Procrastinates—May have difficulty with planning.

- Hands in late assignments—May have difficulty with time management.

- Is easily distracted—May have difficulty with attention.

Treatment Strategies & Tools

- Help child plan by using visual aids as necessary, e.g., lists, outlines, pictures, colors, etc.

- Break down writing tasks into parts, e.g., 1st, 2nd, 3rd, etc.

- Keep workspace organized, minimize clutter, and clearly identify where assignments should be placed when they have been completed.

- Use a timer to monitor time spent on each section of the handwriting assignment.

- Provide a schedule of when assignments are to be completed.

- Use a pencil pouch to improve time management. Include writing tools, e.g., erasers, sharpeners, pencils, pens, highlighters, etc.

- Provide a three-ring binder with subject dividers.

- Encourage the use of self-stick notes for marking pages in a book or jotting down notes.

- Provide graphic organizers, e.g., sequences, story maps, essay writing, flow charts, Venn diagrams, etc.

- Repeat often and practice, practice, practice!!!

Section III
The Driver-Task Performance

To have a pleasant driving experience requires a sturdy and safe road, a well-functioning vehicle, and a competent driver. A competent driver is defined as someone who is familiar with the driving rules, understands them, and executes his/her driving task well.

Handwriting works much the same way. We already learned that legible handwriting is a result of well-developed foundational components and performance skills.

However, legible handwriting can only be produced by a child who is also familiar with the task elements, understands them, has practiced, and is able to execute the handwriting rules.

Handwriting Rules

A child MUST have the CORRECT:

Pencil grasp

Posture

Letter formation

Letter spacing

Letter alignment

Letter directionality

Letter slanting

Letter sizing

Signs of Handwriting Readiness

A child MUST have the following BEFORE he/she is taught handwriting:

- Preferred dominant hand.
- Interest in writing.
- Demonstrable well-developed fine-motor skills.
- Ability to copy simple shapes, like circles and squares.
- Understanding of the concepts of down, up, across, over, under, and the ability to produce these strokes easily.

Chapter 1
Pencil Grasp

It is important for children to know how to hold the pencil properly so that handwriting is legible and produced with the correct speed. Changing a child's pencil grasp works best with young children who have not yet formed a specific hold on the pencil. The correct pencil grasp is known as the Dynamic Tripod Grasp, and it looks like this:

If a child is struggling with holding the pencil correctly, the following strategies and tools may work:

- Provide the child with a pencil grip to encourage a tripod grasp.

- Provide the child with the opportunity to practice writing on a vertical surface, such as an easel or a blackboard.

- Encourage practice, practice, practice of upper-extremity strength/endurance and fine-motor activities (see section II).

For samples of inefficient grasps, see appendix A.

Chapter 2
Writing Posture

The child's desk and chair should allow his/her knees to fit comfortably under the desk and his/her feet to lie flat on the floor. The desk for a left-handed student should be about two inches lower than for a right-handed student. This helps the left-handed student see what he/she has written.

For a right-handed student, the paper is placed directly in front of the student and slanted to the left. The student should place his/her free hand on the top of the paper to keep it steady on the desk. For the left-handed student, the paper is placed in front of the student's left shoulder and slanted to the right. His/her free hand is placed at the top of the paper.

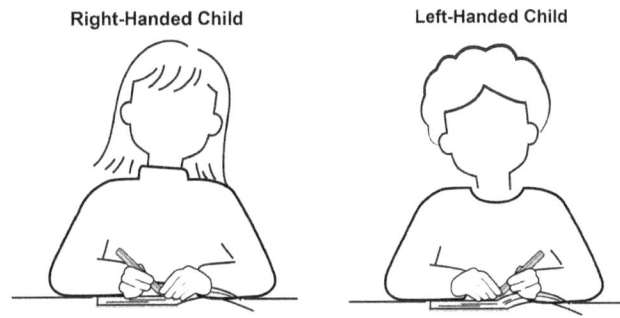

If a child is struggling with posture, the following strategies and tools may work:

- Make sure desk and chair height allow for his/her hips-knees-ankles to be at 90–90–90 degrees.
- Place a foot stool or a stack of books under his/her feet to support them if his/her feet cannot rest flat on floor when seated.
- Work on trunk strength and endurance (see section II).
- Use alternative seating, such as a benches, therapy balls, therapy wedges, and/or standing desks.
- Take frequent rest and movement breaks.

Chapter 3
Handwriting Rules

LETTER FORMATION

Letter Formation refers to the correct way to produce capital and lowercase letters.

- Children first must learn the starting and stopping point of each letter.
- Letters are written left to right and top to bottom. Children do not learn the letters by their shapes, but by their features.
- Rather than teaching the letters in sequential order, teach them in groups.

Short Letters:	a c e i m n o r s u v w x z
Tall Letters:	b d f h k l t
Fall Letters:	g j p q y
Based on C:	a c e s d g o q
Letters with diagonals:	u v w x z y

- Every child has a different learning style; therefore, it is important to use auditory, kinesthetic, and visual approaches to teach letter formation.

Learning correct letter formation from the beginning is important because it will:

- Help the child learn good handwriting habits.

- Minimize b/d/p/q reversal confusion.

- Make smoother the transition from print to cursive.

- Facilitate handwriting development. The older the child gets, the harder it is to get him/her to listen and to correct his/her mistakes.

Correct Letter Formation in Right- Versus Left-Handed Children

Right-handed children produce the letters differently from left-handed children. Right-handed children naturally follow the direction of writing left to right, while left-handed children need to exert extra effort to do so. So, children who are left-handed find it more natural to pull the pencil while forming certain letters from right to left, e.g., A, E, F, G, H, J, L, T, Z.

LETTER ALIGNMENT

Letter Alignment refers to letter placement on lines. For a child to show correct Letter Alignment, he/she must understand the concept of "top" and "bottom" lines. Make this easier by marking the "top line" in one color and the "bottom line" in a different color. When a child has Poor Letter Alignment, letters appear to float over or under the lines.

Example of letters not written on the line:

LETTER SIZING

Letter Sizing refers to letter proportion. Short letters (a, c, e, i, m, n, o, r, s, u, v, w, x, z) should be half the size of both tall letters (b, d, h, k, l, t) and fall letters, which go below the line (g, j, p, q, y). Capital letters should be about the same height as tall letters. Proper proportion can be taught using handwriting paper with a dotted middle line.

A child who has difficulty with Letter Sizing tends to produce letters that are too big, too small, or a mix of both. The letters are inconsistent.

Practice Letter Sizing by making the child aware of these inconsistencies in a nonthreatening manner.

LETTER SPACING

Letter Spacing is having a consistent space or gap between letters and between words. A child with Poor Letter Spacing will combine or overlap words and letters, producing an illegible product. One way to minimize the lack of space between words is to encourage the child to use his/her finger to assist him in establishing proper spacing.

Examples of no spacing between words:

Example of using two fingers to space words:

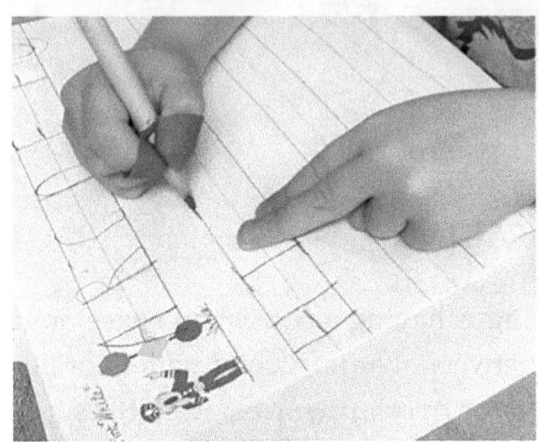

LETTER DIRECTIONALITY

Letter Directionality refers to the handwriting progressing from left to right. Knowing that things go left to right is the foundation for writing, as well as for reading. It is important to know that reversals are fairly common in 5- to 6-year-olds. However, if a child continues to show letter reversals in the 2nd grade, he/she may be suffering from Dyslexia. Commonly reversed letters are **b, d, p, q**.

Example of boy versus yod:

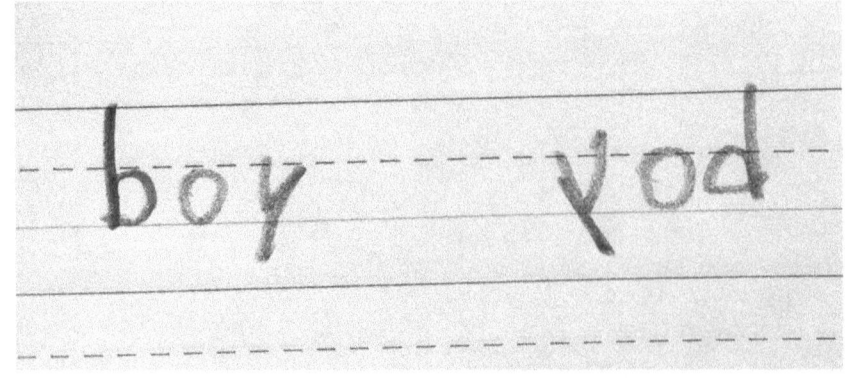

Section IV
Mechanics–When to Seek Further Assistance & From Whom?

How to Determine When to Seek Further Assistance?

Persistent difficulty with handwriting, along with other academic problems, may indicate a necessity for further testing or assistance from an expert.

- Avoidance of pre-writing activities such as scribbling, coloring, drawing, and/or cutting.
- Frustration / avoidance of handwriting, drawing, or copying activities in class/at home.
- Awkward pencil grasp, writes slowly, holds pencil too tightly or too loosely.
- Fatigues quickly during writing/motor tasks.
- Omits letters or words when copying from the board or from the same page.
- Has difficulty naming and/or forming letters and/or numbers.
- Has difficulty remembering sequence and/or reverses letters and/or numbers.
- Has difficulty keeping letter sizing, alignment, spacing between words.

- Easily distracted, fidgety, poor organizational skills and/or emotional regulation.
- The child is bright but struggles with academic work reading, math, spelling, writing thus performs at below grade level expectations.

A common diagnosis for persistent handwriting difficulty may be either Dysgraphia or a Disorder of Written Expression. Dysgraphia is not just "bad" handwriting, but a fancy word for summarizing some combination of weak foundational skills that makes handwriting difficult.

Sometimes you need professionals to help you figure out your child's strengths and weaknesses. They do this through testing. These experts can also give you further guidance on how to improve the area of difficulty, thus making handwriting and overall learning more efficient and less cumbersome.

Some Professionals Who May Prove Beneficial in Diagnosing and/or Treating a Child's Handwriting and/or Academic Concerns

Developmental Pediatrician: Focuses on developmental, behavioral, and learning issues from infancy through young adulthood. They can guide parents as to which services, testing, and/or medications are available to them.

Psychologist: Conducts a psychoeducational evaluation to determine if a diagnosis of Dysgraphia is the culprit. Also establishes if other related diagnoses, e.g., ADHD or Dyslexia, among others, are contributing to a child's handwriting deficits.

Occupational Therapist: Conducts an evaluation to specifically determine the underlying reasons for a child's difficulties with handwriting and then comes up with a treatment plan. Evaluation will be based on a sample of typical written work from school, tasks that assess sensory, motor, visual and fine-motor abilities, and/or standardized tests of writing skills.

Speech Therapist: Conducts an evaluation to determine if a child's expressive language is age appropriate. A child's difficulties with language may affect a child's quality of written expression.

Audiologist: Conducts an evaluation to determine if auditory processing may be affecting a child's overall academic performance.

Developmental Optometrist: Conducts an evaluation to determine if underlying visual issues may be negatively affecting a child's reading, writing, and overall academic performance. The child may be referred for vision therapy if challenges are found to be secondary to vision-related weaknesses.

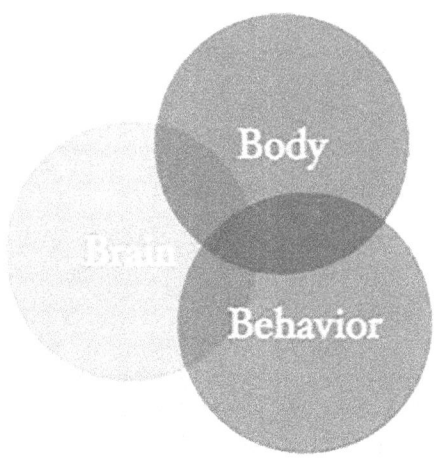

***Disclaimer: Please note that information and activities provided in this guide are designed to promote your child's normal development and are not a substitute for seeking consultations from the above-mentioned specialist(s). If you are concerned about your child's skill development and/or overall learning, please contact an occupational therapist or other professionals as deemed necessary.

Appendix A: Examples of Inefficient Grasps

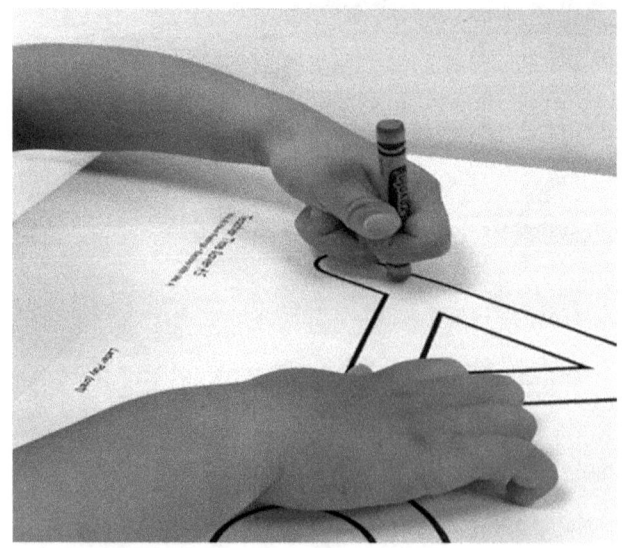

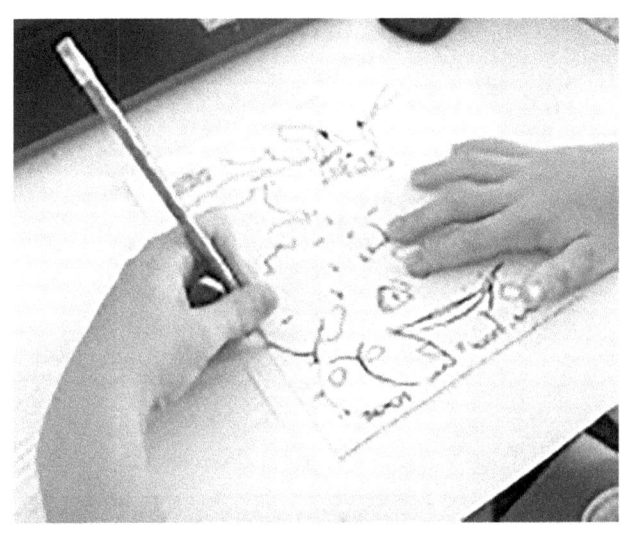

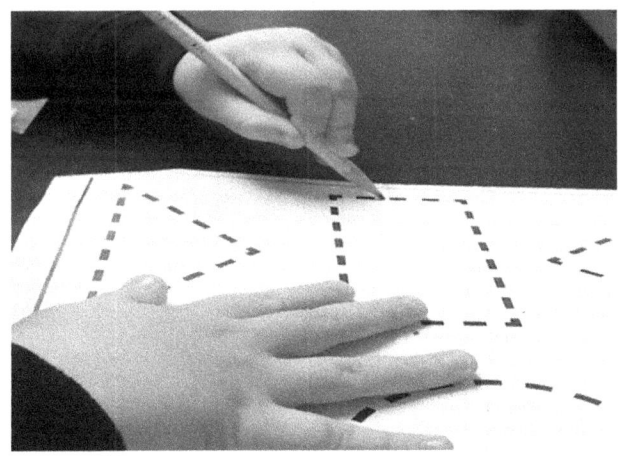

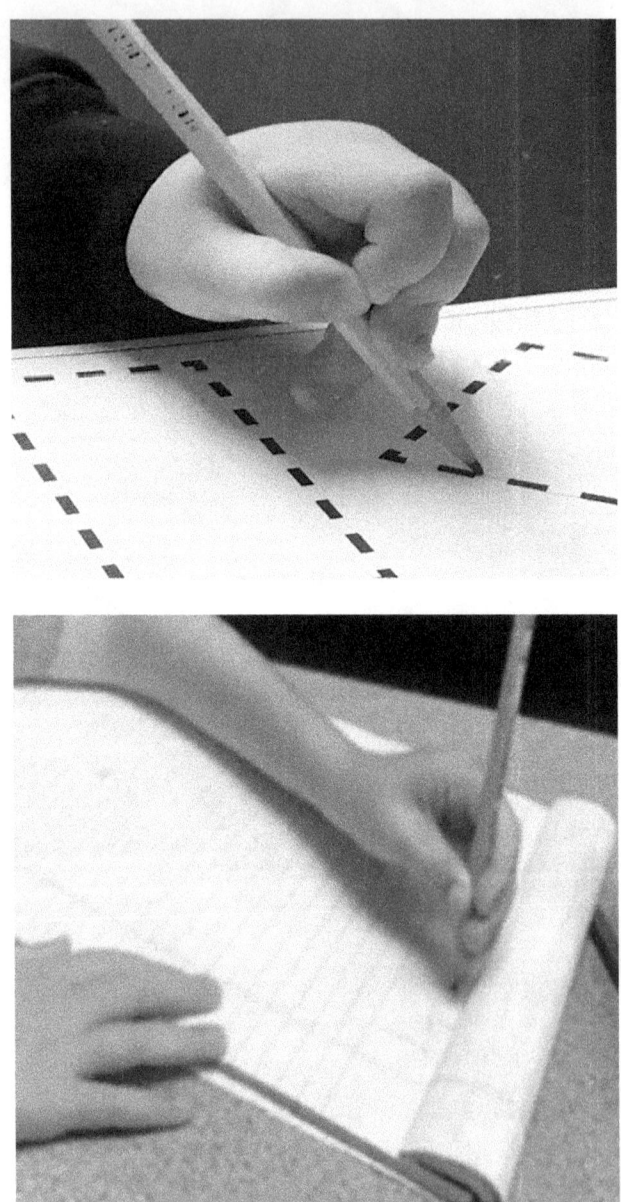

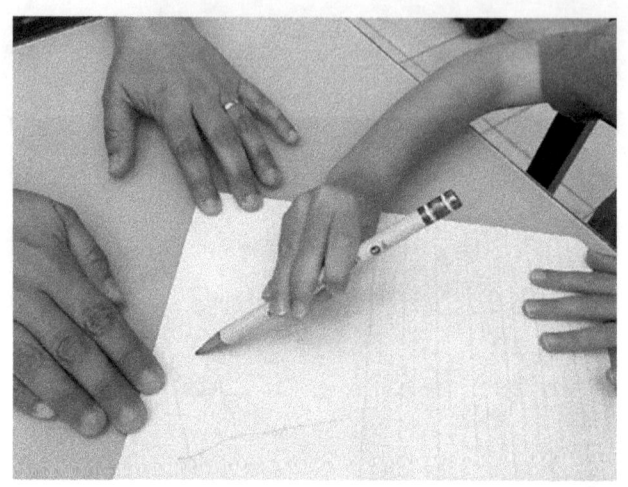
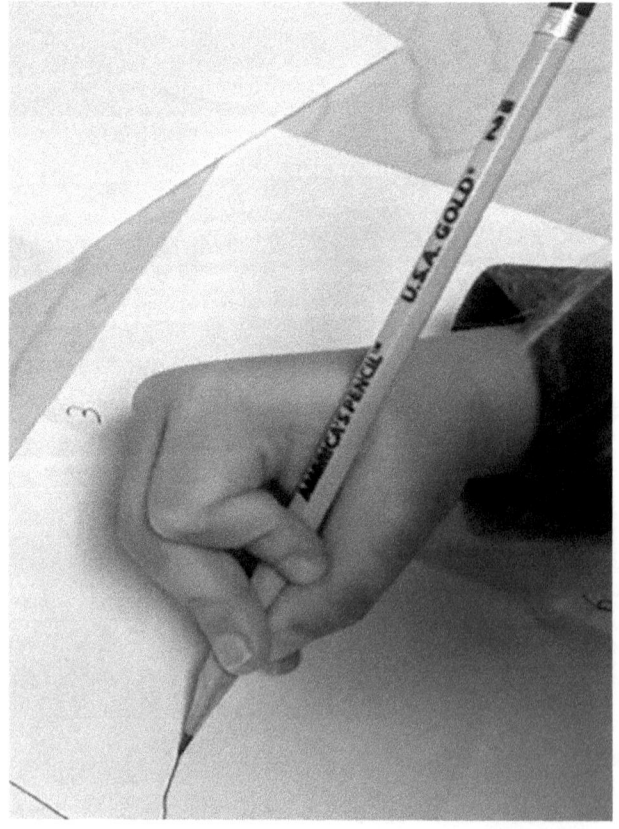

Appendix B: Examples of Handwriting Improvement

Session #1

Session #5

This is a 6.5-year-old child entering 1st grade. This child first presented with poor letter alignment, sizing, formation, and directionality, as well as a dislike for handwriting. Progress is already noted after 4 sessions.

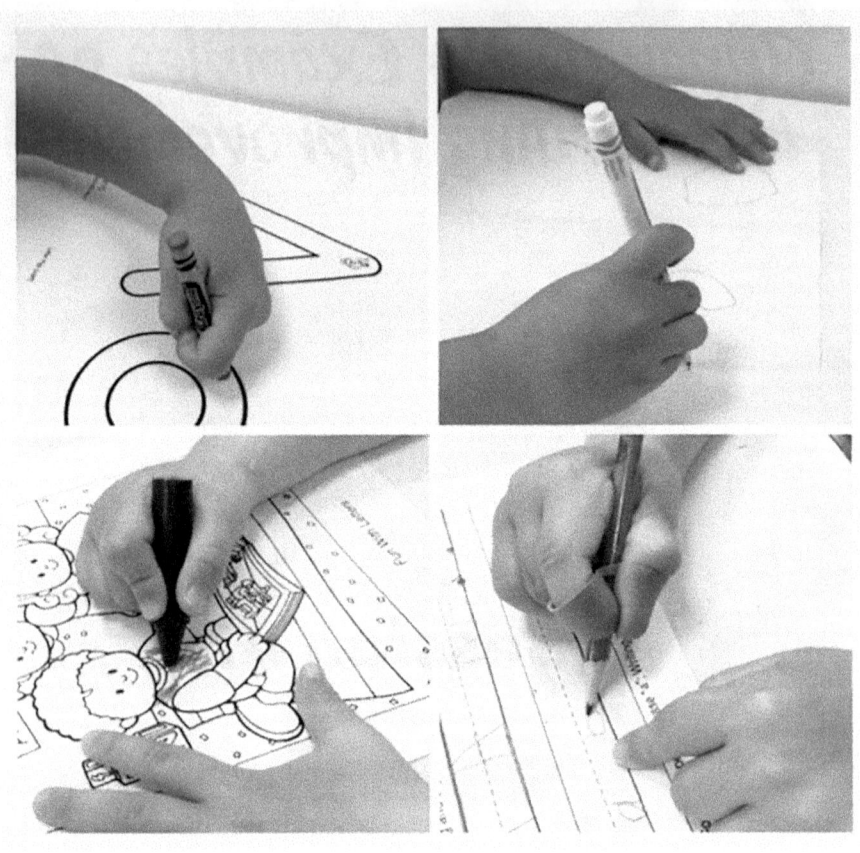

Amazing progress in just 3–4 months.

Top pictures: 3.5-year-old child exhibiting poor grasp, very-light-to-no pressure when using writing/coloring tools, unestablished hand dominance, and decreased confidence in his abilities.

Bottom pictures: Same child with a VERY much improved grasp, confidence, and coloring/writing abilities.

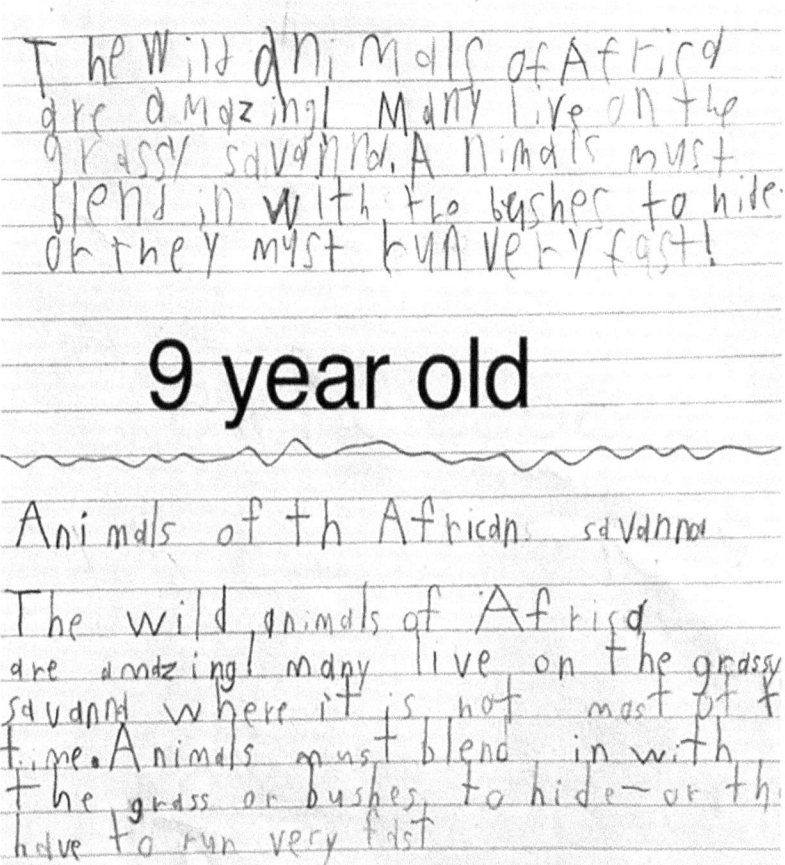

This is a 9-year-old child entering 3rd grade who presented with poor letter alignment, sizing, and formation, as well as a dislike for handwriting. Progress is already noted after 4 sessions.

Session #1

Animals of the african savanna

The wild animals of africa are amazing! Many live on the grassy savanna, where it is hot most of the time. There are not many trees on the savanna. Animals must blend in with the grass and bushes to hide—or they must run very fast!

Session #5

Animals of the african savanna

The wild animals of Africa are amazing! Many live on the grassy savanna, where it is hot most of the time. There are not many trees on the savanna. Animals must blend in with the grass and bushes to hide, or they must run very fast!

12 year old child

This is a 12-year-old child entering 7th grade who presented with poor letter alignment, sizing, formation, spacing, weak grasp, and overall core weakness, as well as a dislike for handwriting. Progress is already noted after 4 sessions.

References

Appelbaum, Stanley, A., O.D. *Sensory Integration: Optometric and Occupational Therapy Perspectives.* **Santa Ana, CA: Optometric Extension Program (DDR), 1989.**

Ayers, A. J. *Sensory Integration, and the Child.* **Los Angeles, CA: Western Psychological Services, 1979.**

Benbow, Mary, M.S., O.T.R. *Loops and Groups: A Kinesthetic Writing System.* **Tucson, AZ: Communication Skill Builders, 1990.**

Fink, Barbara E. *Sensory Motor Integration Activities.* **Tucson, AZ: Therapy Skill Builders, 1989.**

Gardner, Morrison F. *Test of Visual Motor Skills,* revised. **Hydesville, CA: Psychological and Educational Pub, Inc., 1995.**

Haldy, M. and Haack, L. *Making It Easy: Sensorimotor Activities at Home and School.* **Tucson: AZ: Therapy Skill Builders, 1995.**

Hannaford, Carla. *Smart Moves: Why Learning Is Not All in Your Head.* **Arlington, VA: Great Ocean Publishers, Inc., 1995.**

Kranowitz, Carol Stock, M.A. *The Out-of-Sync Child: Recognizing and Coping with Sensory Integration Dysfunction.* **New York, NY: The Berkley Publishing Group, 1998.**

Kranowitz, Carol Stock, M.A. *101 Activities for Kids in Tight Spaces.* **New York, NY: St. Martin's Press (DDR), 1995.**

Gardner, Morrison F.; Brown, G. Ted; Rodger, Sylvia; David, Aileen; and Klein, Sheryl. *Test of Visual Perceptual Skills,* revised. **Hydesville, CA: Psychological and Educational Publications, 1996.**

Olsen, Jan Z. OTR., *Handwriting without Tears.* **Potomac, MD: Handwriting without Tears, Inc., 1998.**

Trott, M. C., Laurel, M., and Windeck, S. L. *SenseAbilities: Understanding Sensory Integration.* **Tucson, AZ: Therapy Skills Builders, 1993.**

Vail, Priscilla L. *Smart Kids with School Problems: Things to Know and Ways to Help.* **New York: Plume Books, 1989.**

Williams, M. S. and Shellenberger, Sherry. *"How Does Your Engine Run?": A Leader's Guide to the Alert Program for Self-Regulation.* **Albuquerque, NM: Therapy Works, Inc. 1996.**

7 Senses Clip Art, Graphics by SayBeluga

All other images produced by author, Dr. Carol Leibovich–Mankes, and Malka Lina

Telephone: (754) 273–5830

Webpage: www.thehandwritingdoctor.com

E-mail: drcarolmankes@gmail.com

About the Author
Dr. Carol Leibovich-Mankes

Dr. Carol Leibovich-Mankes has been an Occupational Therapist and Parent Educator for the past 20 years. She feels strongly about working as a team to develop a healthy and conducive environment of growth for children with developmental delays, learning differences, and/or learning disabilities. Her mission is to assist each child to reach his/her unique and full potential at home, in social settings, and at school.

Dr. Carol Leibovich-Mankes has extensive experience working in private practice and school settings, providing occupational therapy, in addition to parent and health coaching/educational services. She served as adjunct faculty for the Occupational Therapy Master's Program at Nova

Southeastern University's College of Health Care Sciences. She is fluent in English, Spanish, and Hebrew.

Dr. Carol Leibovich-Mankes's educational background includes a Doctorate and Master's Degree In Occupational Therapy from Nova Southeastern University, Bachelor's Degree In Psychology from the University Of Florida, Certification in Grief Counseling and Professional Life, Health, and Parent Coaching.

www.ingramcontent.com/pod-product-compliance
Lightning Source LLC
Chambersburg PA
CBHW071737090426
42738CB00011B/2510